Unforgettable

MADALINA COMAN

ROMANTIC QUOTES, POETRY AND POETIC PROSE

UNFORGETTABLE
WRITTEN AND ARRANGED BY MADALINA
COMAN

www.instagram.com/madalinacoman

www.facebook.com/madalina.poetry

www.twitter.com/mada_c

Cover Illustration by Beatriz Mutelet
Interior Illustrations by Beatriz Mutelet

www.instagram.com/beatriz_mutelet

Cover Design by Mitch Green
Interior Design by Mitch Green

www.instagram.com/mitch_grn

DEDICATION

These words are to be shared with anyone who needs to read them. These words are to be held close to your chests and felt; they are not absolute truths, they are mere invitations to forgiveness and love. If they feel like warm blankets in the middle of winter, feel free to wrap yourselves in them and keep them...if they become daggers reaching too deep into your hearts, feel free to dispose of them.

These words are here for you,
if you choose to offer them a home.

To my children:
You taught me more about love in a few seconds of life, than most people did in decades. Because of you, I strive to be a better person...every single day. I hope you never forget how much I love you! You are the light of my eyes...and that will never change...And if you ever read this book, I hope you remember to never give up on love, no matter how hard feeling might seem at times.
You are the loves of my life! I love you!

We all have memories that are sacred to us, that we have kept for ourselves. They bridge our pasts and our present. Some of these are sources of great beauty and we hold them dear. Others bring pain and heartache, and these we often wish to forget.

In life, however, the darkness and the light are of equal importance. We must embrace the totality of the human experience – even the difficult, ugly, and messy parts. Great awakenings can come from loving and losing, but only if we are willing to stand in the storms of all the exquisite highs and agonizing lows of life.

'Unforgettable' is a searing and exhilarating journey along the winding path of memory. The poems, romantic quotes and poetic prose in this book are grounded in an eternal present, lifting the reader out of the ordinary concepts of love and into the extraordinary. The stories and concepts pull apart and recombine like shining rivers, blending love, dreams and reality. The reader is invited to link arms with the writer and step into a celebration of love, forgiveness, and a final acceptance.

Foreword

Madalina Coman is a healer, whose words inspire the lives of anyone fortunate enough to come across her work. Her poetry delves deep into the human psyche-- touching on themes of love, grief, and the memories that tuck themselves away in the innermost areas of our hearts and minds.

Madalina puts words to all things unseen: the emotions that perplex us, the intricacies involved in relationships, and the thoughts we rarely share aloud. To engage with her work is to be comforted and encouraged; to heal is to let her words sink into the most wounded parts of your soul.

Delicately but profoundly, Madalina takes readers on a journey, reminding us that as human beings we are beautiful, we are complex, but most importantly-- we are never truly alone in this world.

Molly S. Hillery, Author of 'bare roots'

Welcome

Whether you are holding this book in your hands because you intentionally purchased it or whether you somehow came upon finding it somewhere: *welcome and thank you for being here!* I don't believe we ever stumble upon books accidentally. *I believe that books find us;* there is a part of us in need of whatever the book we pick up or we receive as a gift has to offer. And so, whatever the reason my book found its way into your life, I hope it brings you what you need.

When I started writing this book, my intention was to write about a utopian kind of love; the love I have always dreamt of, ever since I was a little girl and thoughts of romantic love entered my heart. I wanted my children to one day pick up this book and believe in the beauty of a perfect love. I wanted them to not get stuck on the painful aspects of love and harden themselves in the process. My intent was pure and came from a place of deep care and protection. However, as I was putting the book together, I realized that by picking and choosing which of my experiences to display in this book, I was doing nothing else but setting them up for failure. Too many books already paint an idealized view of love and I did not want this to be another one of those. Instead, I wanted this book to be a genuine representation of my own experiences with love and how I managed to maintain a soft and tender heart in spite of all that I have been through.

Understanding the trials and tribulations of love is an essential part of fulfilment in life. I am not saying that there needs to be suffering in order to appreciate a special moment. What I am saying is that we often have an idealized image of love with which we enter a relationship and we are so blinded by the initial fireworks, that we do not realize a relationship in order to last, needs a lot more. Relationships need work and hard work in relationships is not for everyone. So, when you meet someone who is willing to put in the work, after having met so many others who were either not ready or willing to invest and commit, something magical happens. And then, sometimes, love takes a while to reach us, while other times, it forgets about us all-together. It is then up to us to learn to integrate forgiveness and acceptance into our lives in order to keep pushing forward, while never losing hope.

This book is not a journey towards anything while being a journey through everything. There is no linearity in it and it is not divided into chapters, because love is messy and unpredictable. One cannot dive into the deep waters of love expecting to come out without a scratch.

Grief after losing love comes in waves. Today it could teach you about the push to forget, while tomorrow it could bring a valuable lesson about the pull to remember...All the while bringing you closer and closer to the call your heart is putting into the Universe to one-day love again.

This book is a very raw piece of my heart put onto paper. And because it is a window into my soul, I ask of you to please wipe your feet clean as you enter my world...maybe leave your shoes and ego at the door. You might not resonate with everything in it and that is completely okay. Keep in mind, you and I are different people, with different histories, experiences and lenses through which we see the world. However, as with most experiences, you will get from this... whatever you put in. *My invitation is to open your heart and let my words guide you...*This is a rollercoaster you are embarking on. After having waited in line for so long, you are finally getting on it. There will be moments of excitement, and there will be moments when your heart might be broken to pieces...my hope as you ride this rollercoaster...is that you will be willing to let your hair down and throw your hands up in the air from time to time...Let yourself be...

We each move through suffering differently and at our own
pace.
There should be no expectations put on our heart about
a right way to move through hurt. *The only right way is*
your own way! Move through it the way that makes sense
the most for you, while keeping in mind that feeling is
nothing to be ashamed of...no matter what that feeling
is. Extend acceptance to your heart for whatever it needs
today and allow yourself to
be surprised by what tomorrow brings. Feeling is purely
proof that you have maintained your humanity; it does
not speak to how behind you are on anything. Give
yourself the gift of feeling as so many others have severed
their bodies from it and are now working hard on getting
rid of the numbness and getting re-acquainted with their
own feelings. There is no moving forward from pain by
pushing feelings away!
The only way forward, the only way towards healing is through
feeling!
I hope you never forget this!

My hope is that through this book you understand
that when it comes to love, the association between feelings
and memories is a beautiful one and even when it is a painful
experience, all it does is remind you that you have kept your
humanity in spite of how harsh life has been on you!

Your softness, your tenderness is a gift...not just to yourself
and the people close to you, but to the world!

This book is to be savored with your feet up and a glass of good wine or curled in an armchair, with soft blankets warming your feet, while sipping on hot cocoa in the middle of a cold day.

As always, you have my gratitude for following my journey, as I have struggled with putting expectations on my heart over what to feel and how to feel my entire life. I have also struggled with guilt coming from painful memories and it took me years to realize that *nothing was a waste*. Whatever was felt, served a higher purpose, years after the experiences ended.

I hope this book helps you to find it within you to believe in love again and to answer its call when it will reach its hand out to you again!

Much Love,
Madalina

your
memory,
walks in
on me,
uninvited,
whenever
it wants.

I write,

    because it hurts too much to hold it all inside. We go through life rewarded for how well we regulate our emotions. We constantly get praised when we seem in control of things. Nobody teaches us how to sit with our emotions. We are made to feel needy, defective, faulty… for feeling too much. Nobody is brave enough to admit the special quality of being an empath. There is strength in feeling…

    because without writing I would have no self. I would have to swallow the vastness of these tears that well up in my eyes as I'm driving and a song that reminds me of you comes on…

    because writing opens a window of connection with others feeling the same way that I do and suddenly, I don't feel so inadequate, so alone in my struggle anymore.

I write of *you*
so
I wouldn't write
to *you.*

When was the last time you allowed your heart to truly feel? And I am not talking about warm, fuzzy feelings that end up inspiring Hollywood romances. I am talking about the darkness; the destruction that follows after a heart gets broken and the tendency we have to run away and not confront the pain. The more we run from it, the more it starts eating away at our days, our relationships and our future. We can't escape the things we have not felt. We can't put Band-Aids on wounds that were not allowed to bleed as much as they needed to. So, before you wonder why you cannot move on, why you cannot let go, you need to think of the last time shivers of pain entered and existed your heart's cracks like lava leaving trails of destruction wherever it traveled. Some things need to be burnt to the ground before they can shape-shift into something glorious again.

Don't ask for permission from anyone to fall apart. Just fall. Crumble. It doesn't have to be pretty, but it has to be real. Make it safe enough for you to bring on the flood tonight, because come morning, a warrior will rise with the first rays of sunshine.

And this is how it starts: the initial shock of messages that stop coming, phone calls that seem so far removed, you end up questioning whether they were even real after all; maybe you dreamt the whole thing from the beginning. Think of the initial shock of losing the person who once meant everything to you in terms of losing a hand, an arm, a leg. At first it seems inconceivable. Gone are the dreams of you ever playing the piano with just one hand. Gone are the ideas of running your first marathon with just one leg; and in the same way, think of dreams of happiness, vacations to Italy – sipping coffee early in the morning in Tuscany right before a short summer rain starts, when there is just a small window of time available to sneak a kiss in the rain, before the sun takes over again – they are all gone. Gone are the walks around Seine where he looks into your eyes and without saying a word, he tells you exactly what you want to hear. Gone. Because what good is anything without sharing it with the only person in the world who takes your breath away and makes your heart stop and start between kisses? What good is living a life that does not make you feel alive? and then one day, just the way you slowly adjust to the death of a loved one, you adjust to losing him. You never actually forget him. A love like that cannot possibly be forgotten and if one day you end up saying you did, you either never loved him the way you thought you did, or you were trying to deceive yourself. A love like that lives on. But you learn to live without it, just the way you learn to live without a hand or a leg. And little by little the memories seem more and more distant, until one day, when you can barely taste them anymore.

And yet, whenever it rains, you still look up at the clouds and wonder if you are ever going to see him again, even if it is just so you may share one last kiss, on a rainy morning in Tuscany.

the most heartbreaking sound
you will ever hear
can be heard
in the footsteps of the person you love
walking away from you.

running away from
all memories of you,
all the emotions drowning my heart,
all the sensations breaking my body;

always running away from the pain
of remembering too much.

so much running,
is not good for the heart.

I wish
forgetting
was something
I was good at.

I have become
an anthology
of memories
of you.

when love dies
we are quick to blame it on

time,
distance,
circumstances

before we have the courage
to acknowledge
that at the end of the day,

people do change.

We spend our lives, lying to ourselves.
When we are in a relationship, we are not in love with the person we're with. There is this tiny little hope banging on the door from time to time exciting us with the idea of how much more we could love this person if only they changed this or that about themselves. Nothing major. We still love them at their core, but if they could only address these tiny little things. Wow. How much more fun they would be to live with. When relationships don't work out, we start another round of lies. It wasn't the right time. It wasn't the right person. It wasn't the right place. It just wasn't right. But maybe...just maybe...the next person is going to be different...And a new cycle of lies starts.

We are older now, so we are more experienced, and our lies get better. We are more convincing: both at convincing other people of how defective they are and at convincing ourselves that life is unfair and we are constant victims of a broken system.

We are close to death and we realize we've been waiting for love our entire lives...the right kind of love...the right time to find it...the right place to find it in...We've been waiting for it to find us our entire lives and when we realize we could have done more to go find it ourselves... we can't anymore...because there is no more time. The casket is calling our name...We've spent our lives living in little bubbles of the past...stuck in memories we missed and longed to get back...and from time to time we peeked our heads out and visualized an idealized future...while the present...The present stood in disbelief and watched us all along not paying any attention to it...Never minding its presence...never once taking it seriously... Never acknowledging the many opportunities that it was carrying for us.

We leave this world with our mouths closed...interrupted mid-sentence by another lie looking to make its way up into the air and promise us things will be different on the other side...

We are lured into after-life by the many promises that death comes to offer...

And we never stop lying to ourselves...Not in life,
not in death...not even in nothingness.

it was
on a day like today
calm, yet tasting of
fall and farewell,
on a bench in Pacifica
looking at the ocean
while your hand
traced the back of my spine
underneath a white cotton shirt,
that I looked love in the eyes
and it looked back at me.
longingly.
lovingly.
tragically tearing up.
knowing that was going to be,

the last time we would ever meet.

ever since you've left,
I've found myself in
a long-distance relationship
with
my own heart.

you were
my refuge from
inner emptiness;
ironically,

you left with both
your fullness and mine.

like a thief,
you were breaking
and entering,
stealing
my heart's essence.

the taste of hope on my lips,
always made him
take a step back.
while I,
saw things in his eyes
he was unable
to see himself.
but,

I had to quiet my heart
for it was not my place
to teach him about feelings.

staring at the screen of a phone for hours. wanting to write something, but having no idea where to start and what to say. how do we get from not finding enough time to share everything we want to share with the person we love, to not even being able to muster one suitable word to start a conversion with?

where do our words go when our hearts get broken? who steals them and where do they hide them? how do we get them back?

do we ever get them back?

we might have felt
the same thing,
but only one of us
was brave enough
to put it into words.

maybe one day,
these tears will stop.
maybe after this winter,
they won't feel as if
they need to stick around
and keep my cheeks warm.
and then again,
maybe they won't.
as I keep waiting for them to
leave
and every season,
of every year,
they are still here,

and I,
am still in love.

Time heals all wounds.

Every time someone doesn't know how to help, what to say, what to do...Every time someone feels incompetent when faced with a loved one's pain, they will open their big mouths and with astronomic confidence, will utter those four little words. As if, suddenly they stumbled upon the miracle cure: one that is sure to cure you, but also take away from their incompetence.

Time heals nothing.

If you are stuck in a bubble of suffering, time will not stop to untie your knots and unravel your pain. Time will pass right by you and you will continue to be stuck and suffer.

**Time heals, when you allow it
to pass through you.**

Time heals when you are ready to acknowledge your pain and sit with it. Time doesn't plead with you. Time is not there to convince you to face your doubts and your fears.

**Time heals when you choose
to show up for your pain.**

**Time doesn't heal, unless you're ready to
acknowledge that there is work to be done and that
you are ready and willing to start.**

what can I call
the rest of my days,
since without you,

this,
cannot be called
a life?!

some loves,
leave a trail of bodies
disposed off
on the side of the road
right after that last goodbye.

others,
invite you in,
make you a cup of warm tea
and beg you to stay for the night.

in love,
you have to come prepared,
with both
your personal body bag
and your extra toothbrush
and change of clothes,

for you never know which type of love
is going to claw its way into your heart
come sunrise.

what I once loved,
what made you special,
is a thing of the past.
you were the face of sunny days
and wild flowers
breaking through concrete
and other unlikely places.
now,
you are nothing more than,

the feel of open wounds,
knots stuck down my throat
and the taste of
broken promises.

he left me
the way one leaves
an obedient dog
wagging its tail
watching its master
close the door behind him
and move about his day
and there,
I remained

waiting and wondering
when he'd be back.

I think
there's something to be said about
the way you take me whole
dig your hands
into the core of my being
and pull out pieces
leaving me
shattered
my pieces
scattered

and
for others
to put me back
together.

he was
both love and heartbreak
all at once.

there's this entire life
I've lived with you
in my head,

that no one
knows about.

it feels
as if
I've been
lost at sea
for centuries

waiting

for your heart
to walk
towards me
with conviction
and intention.

when your world
feels like is ending,
remember
how many times before
it has ended at sundown,
only to be revived
in the gentlest of ways
by the warmth
of the very first rays
of sun
during sunrise.

and that's the problem with love:

we complain
when we don't have it.
we exhaust ourselves
in order to find it.
we don't know
how to appreciate it
when we get it.
and when it's over,
and we're hurting
we wish it would be
as easy to slip off
as our favorite piece
of black lingerie.

but love,
doesn't answer to anyone.
it comes and goes
when and as it pleases.

some of us
spend a lifetime
looking for true love,
while others
stumble upon it
accidently
and then discard it
without giving it
a second thought
or ever realizing
its value.

I loved you,
the way
I craved to be loved by you;
not realizing that maybe,

you needed to be loved
differently.

our hearts
were too wild
to miss each other
in this tame universe,

*they never really
stood a chance.*

you and I,
were never meant
for the eyes of the world.
we were only meant,

to love each other
behind closed doors.

within you,
I heard whispers
of temptation and sin.
and like ribbons
of seductive silk
I felt them tie themselves
in knots of promises
around my heart.

And if you were to ask me when I fell in love with you, I wouldn't know where to begin. You were an unexpected guest in my world. But if I had to guess, it could have very well been the warmth of the train story from your childhood that set my heart on fire. Your words serenaded a song I recognized from long ago. Another proof that I had known you from a time I cannot properly recall. A time when my heart knew how to love without the need to be guarded. You melted my walls and I didn't even have time to notice it. *Before I knew it, I was already yours.* I held your words tightly and to this day, I remember their melody like a healing ballad of soulful medicine. The strength of your embrace that night, your heart beating in unison with mine, your eyes glimmering with the hope and excitement of new love, and a calm I had never felt before – it was somewhere in the middle of this all that I fell in love.

You were the first thing I didn't feel I needed to run from, but rather, run towards. You were what words are made for, but never able to describe. You were my forever, turned yesterday.

the mornings
you can't look at yourself
in the mirror
because
you can't recognize
the cloudy, teary eyes
staring back at you,
are the best mornings
to remind yourself of
the immense power of healing
only found within.

forgiveness is a gift
you gift yourself
and it should come
in your own time
and on your own terms.

forgive because you're ready
and not because
you're asked to.

whisper love into ears
that have stopped
believing in kindness
and watch them
turn
their attention
towards your voice
like tiny antennae
trying to decode
encrypted messages
coming from unknown channels
whose language
was long thought
to be forgotten.

love her
when she needs it
the most,
not when
it is the most convenient
for you.

settling,
is death to
a beating heart.

we don't fall in love
with the person.
we fall in love
with the potential in a person.
we don't fall in love
with the present.
we fall in love with the future
we see in their eyes,
taste on their lips
and feel
on their skin.

everyone

wants someone

while they,

want someone else.

come,
take my hand
and lay your head
on my breasts.
I promise
I'll help you
forget her,
if you promise to

help me
remember him.

you grew roots
in the most unexpected of places
in the core of my soul.
I've been trying to pull you out
with both hands,
but you keep resisting me.
you keep breaking through,

like a wild flower
breaking through concrete.

write me,
in the stars
of your heart.
for those

will shine bright
long after we're gone.

not everyone
is here for the long run.
some are just interested in
dipping their toes in the water.
and as soon as they discover
you are the ocean,
suddenly
they become seasick.

Sometimes we become so stubborn, so set on wanting to see something in someone that we miss seeing the reality of the situation. We bury our heads in a cocoon of distortions because making peace with reality and accepting our current situation would hurt too much. So, we sip on hope every time we feel ourselves getting a taste of reality and that's how we keep ourselves drunk on mere dreams and illusions that have very few chances of materializing into something tangible, something real one day.

You *see..I was different*. I did not give up when things got tough. I tried to understand what the problem was. I tried to put things into perspective and find a way not only to get us back on track, but also to find a durable solution so the problem wouldn't later on re-emerge. I did not like the idea of using temporary methods to stop deep wounds from bleeding. I was ready to go to battle for us. I wasn't in it for the short-run. I never expected it to be easy. I came in hoping that it would be hard, so I may show you all the ways in which I was prepared to fight for us. All the ways in which I loved you. Not only when things were easy, but particularly when things got hard. Maybe if I had been more selfish, played more games, I wouldn't be the one lying depleted on the side of the road.

I was different and that scared you.

not everything
we feel or see,
is as real as
we perceive it to be.

some people
are just better
at wearing their masks,
for a little while longer
than most.

I don't think there's ever
a good time
to say goodbye
to someone.

and

I don't think
there's ever
a right way to go
about saying it, either.

don't promise her
tomorrow,
when you could give her
today.

you can't make people
see the light,
no matter how much
the sun is shinning.

they have to
be willing to see it themselves
otherwise,

they'll only end up
blinded by it.

I don't make love in armchairs anymore
and I've stopped wearing heels in bed, too.
I have not tasted cookies and cream ice cream
since the last time I licked whatever was left
on your spoon.
I had an interview not too long ago by where you used
to live. The place is now remodeled.
It seemed to have moved on, much like you did.
While I…
I am still learning how to live today
without dragging you and all our yesterdays
into my future.

And in case you ever wonder, I still have days when I wake
up, grab my coat, the keys to my car and as I walk through the
door, I remember there's no longer a YOU I can surprise
with an early morning kiss before the world wakes up…
You are gone…You have moved on…
And I'd better move on, too…

As you're grieving the loss of his love,
make your heart safe enough for you
to start loving yourself again.

he asserts

with so much certainty

that the last thing

he would ever want to do

is hurt me.

yet,

he pushes my head under water

every time

he makes me feel forgotten.

and then

he pulls me up

by the hair

so I could get

just enough air

with a hello

and a 'how you've been',

once in a while

and completely

on a whim.

never go to bed
wearing anger
on your shoulders
or in your chest.
close your eyes
and imagine yourself
draped
in love and gratitude
from head to toes.
go to bed
with your heart
full of compassion
and notice your soul
feeling
weightless
by morning.

I didn't need his lips
to utter
those three little words,
while we were together.
his eyes did more talking
than he ever knew.
but when he left,

I started missing the words...

now that you're gone,

we speak

in memories and after-tastes.

and I can still

feel you

vibrating

within the confines

of this body

as if,

you had never left

the comfort of my arms.

and somehow
tomorrow became
next week,
next month,
next year.
and in a heartbeat
a decade passed

you are still there.
and I am still here...

what can I do
when
you open your mouth
and I believe
everything
that rolls off
your tongue?

-empty promises

I've loved you
for so long,
I've forgotten
what it feels like
not to love you.

you were
my unsung song,
my unwritten poem

until
you became
everything I write about.

you could find her heart
passionately hugging
memories of him
as if it depended on them
for survival.
just the way her legs
locked tightly around his body
every time they made love
with no intention of
ever letting go.

-for this was the only way
she knew how to love

Come as you are. Yes, with all that is troubling you. With all this anger stuck between your teeth threatening to turn to ruin everything around you like lava spilling out of an active volcano. With all the sadness that like an octopus with endless arms was pulling you back into bed this morning. With all the anxiety living in your chest and like an anchor is bringing you down lower and lower every day. With the negative self-talk that's built a nest in your head. With the fears and the doubts that you've packed in that old backpack you carry around on your shoulders, which feels heavier than all the river rocks you ever threw as a kid in the water combined.

Come as you are. Don't wait for the waves to pass and then find me. Together we'll unpack all that is troubling you right now and one by one they will leave your heart, your mind and your life. You don't have to do this alone. Don't wait to improve in any way. Just don't wait. Come to me as you are and I shall receive you right now, for you already are everything you've always wanted to be. You already are, everything I've wanted out of this world…out of this life…We already are all the fairytales we've ever dreamed about love.

Come as you are. You are loved and you are welcomed here.

there was
laughter inside of you,
sadness in your eyes,
adventure in your heart,
and sweet sin on your lips.

I just didn't know
where to begin.

I took it all in
and loved you
all at once.

I saw

cities in his eyes,

lying neglected in the dark.

can you blame me

for trying to bring them

some light?

I don't know how
to say "no"
to a man
I've always said
"yes" to.

out of all
the thoughts
that have ever
tempted me
you
were the only one
I could never resist to.

it wasn't
that I
couldn't
let him go.

it was
he
who pulled me
back in,

every time
he felt me
slipping away.

even

with an ocean

between us,

your heart

still speaks to me.

there are echoes
of "what if"
resounding in each
and every one
of my tomorrows.

on the nights

with restless skies,

I often wonder

whether

your heart

is restless with regret, too.

I've got taste-buds
buried under my skin,
waiting for your return.
with every sunrise,
they peek-through

like sunflowers
looking for the sun.

I know
you will return to me one day,
wrapped in sunshine
and delicate daffodils,
a morning gift
presented by spring
as remembrance
of things past.

stars,
cracked in your chest
at the sight of my eyes

and you'd like me to believe
that
wasn't love?

a sky full of stars
yet, they all fade
when the only thing
that you want
is the moon.

almost 8 billion people
yet, the earth feels
destitute
when the seat next to me
is empty of you.

It feels new, surreal even, when you tell me what I mean to you. When things that I only dreamt to hear from you one day, slowly make their way into the space between us and I wish I could let them sink in. I wish there was a way I could rejoice in hearing you say I have ruined it for every single woman who is trying to make her way into your heart. I have ruined it because none will ever make you feel so loved, so understood, so important, irresistible & worthy of love...And I wish there was a way for me to welcome all this newness into my heart. After all, I have been waiting to hear these words...of affirmation, words of validation, words of love and lust and desire and intimacy, but mostly, words of vulnerability...for years and years and years. And every time I took a step towards you, you were taking two steps back. Every time an "I love you" slipped out of my mouth, it never mended anything. It never healed or made it safe for you to return it in kind. It always made you feel pushed, to do the same...And now...after all these years...when there are no more "I love you"s slipping out of me...You come to me with words that only dreams are made of. You come to me with an openness and an honesty I have yet to learn to associate with you. And all I do is silence myself. And push back. I wish I could take all this beauty and warmth in. For my sake. For your sake. For the sake of this love that seems to find us, no matter how many thousands of miles we put in-between us. I wish I could. But with all the pain, the maybes, the unreliability of our past...with all your incertitude, your guilt, your inability to share yourself with me the way I had shared myself with you...With all our past pouring into our present and all our unfinished business and unresolved issues...

...Walls of doubt are being built all around me whenever something too kind...and just a little too dreamy makes its way into the space between us...
I wish I could...but I can't... it is not that I won't;
it is simply that you have never made it safe enough for me to feel.

my arms,
will never tire
of waiting
for your embrace.

still waiting for you –
somewhere on the edge of yesterday,
hoping that
we could go back,

to a time
before it was too late.

time passes

seasons change
feelings change
people change

yet,

our love remains
the same.

between us
there will always be
too much love
and

not enough distance
to keep us apart.

through the stars,
the moon and
infinite dreams,
by morning,
I always find
my way back
to you.

parting my lips,
a feeling of yearning
took over
as I recalled
being curled up
in your arms,
so close that
I could never tell,

where my breath ended
and yours began.

you remind me
of everything
I miss in this world.

you're both.
the sun
that lights up my soul
and the rain,
that puts out the fires
in my heart.

you,
were missed
before
I even knew
your name.

the closer I get to you,
the more elusive
you become.

I'm a wanderer
and perhaps one day
this gypsy heart of mine
is going to wander
into your heart again.

I've learned
to live
in two places at once:
where I am
and then,
where you are.

for my body sleeps in my bed,
but, my mind travels to you
all night.

I didn't know
how to keep you.

and now,

I don't know
how to let you go.

how strange,
to wake to you;
even though,
you're never here.

a little piece of sunshine,
forever dancing
on my skin.

-the memory of you

I long for you
just like the seed,
buried
deep into the ground
is longing for

its very first taste
of water.

in my mind,
our thoughts
are still
making love
to each other.

on a bare branch
in my thoughts
there is a space
waiting to be filled,
with all moments
never caught
in the net of time,

never experienced
between you and I.

.

you are
the missing piece
in the jigsaw
of my life.

all these lines
making their way
onto paper,

are tears
my heart squeezes
out of herself,

in her last efforts
to hold onto
what used to be you.

Falling in love with you, was reminiscent of the concept of quantum entanglement in the field of quantum mechanics: there was a feeling of inevitability when we met...as if...that cold December night, was not the first time we had interacted with one another. As if we had vibrated in unison, at least once, before having been separated. We emerged from being a collection of elementary particles engaged in a cosmic dance, into something that now defies logic and reason. Our souls never knew why they were so drawn to one another. All we knew was that we always yearned to be close to each other, no matter how much time passed and how many miles stretched between your heart and mine...as if...something beyond our control was calling us to reunite. Our everyday sense of separation seemed more an illusion than a reality, for I could always feel the fabric of your being within my soul calling you to return home. It is said that cells in the body destroy and renew every seven years; then, how come, after decades, I reach my hand to search for you, like I always do this time of the year...and what I can feel as my fingers touch the air... is not something foreign or forgotten, but rather this familiar unfurling of wild in my bones looking for you wherever I go.

Our lives, just like our bodies, were fated to converge again and again and again. And it doesn't bother me that I'll spend eternity chasing you through time and space in hopes of another cosmic dance.

we must be honest
with ourselves
and I lied to my heart
every time I promised
I'd forget you
knowing all too well,

I never will.

I know
how to ignite fires
where there was only
numbness once.
and once I see those flames
swinging proudly in the wind
like freedom flags,
I fall in love.
and I can't for the life of me
see them being put out again.

I don't know how to let them go.

it has always been you

even when
I did not want to see it,
even when
I did not want to admit it,
across time and distance
it has always been you.
and

it will always be you
my heart will
return to.

you can't let go
of someone you expect
to come back

and

you can't forget
someone you fight so hard
to remember.

tulips,
have blossomed
from every single crack
you left in my heart.
and when it rains,
they all close up
to take in
just one last breath

of the perfume
that was us.

All the waiting in this world, all the patience, the understanding, the mountains of love you extend... all of it is not enough to make someone ready for a relationship, for commitment. The same way, all the ultimatums you keep giving them are not going to serve as a push towards light. They will only push them into an even deeper kind of darkness. If they are not ready today, no matter what you do, they will not be ready tomorrow. **Readiness to enter and stay in a relationship comes from inner work. Without inner work, there is no inner shift.** Sometimes we are tired of waiting...tired of giving second chances...tired of wasting our time with relationships that are not reciprocated in effort, time and love. And so, after having been patient for so long, we want to feel like we matter...like our time has not been wasted and our efforts have not been in vain. And so, we lash out. We become something we don't recognize anymore. And we become confused. How can the person I love most in the world bring both the best and the worst out of me? How can I be both the one he cannot live without and the one he cannot be around all at the same time? Love does that to hearts, to people. **Love brings out both the darkness and the light...the patience and the impulsivity...the trials and the victories...**And that is what makes love such a rare and exquisite experience. Once you have loved in this manner, you are forever changed; it is as if your heart has expanded to reach a size never seen before. And what is most poignant in this process is that once expanded, a heart can never go back to being small again. From here on now, it can only grow bigger, wiser, more beautiful and magical.

And in the end...the coming and the going...the waiting... the breaking...none of it was ever in vain or ever time wasted ... because through it all, you grew into something so soft, so tender and ever so beautiful. You grew into yourself in a way that only love can make you grow.

what lulled me to sleep last night,
was not the sound of my tears
gently echoing your name,
as they were making love
to my cheeks.

what lulled me to sleep last night,
was the sound of my broken heart,
whispering words of forgiveness
for having put her through so much,
when I had no right.

love stories,

are sealed with *"always"*

ours,

never made it past *"almost"*.

as I'm standing
on the shoulders of time
to revisit my life
I remember there used to be magic in us
in the way I would think of
your fingers belonging interlaced in mine.
in the future we would together one day find
in all the places we would travel
never alone and always together
in all those lazy Sundays of

     every week

     every month

     every season

when all we needed was
a meaningful kiss for a reason
to never get out of bed
to never let go of
each other again.

I am old and you are gone
and there is no more time
for us to live that life.

While I love lilies of the valley for their innocence and hope-giving quality, I never wanted to be the one who planted a simple flower that bloomed every spring in your heart. the lilies were never able to truly describe the intensity that lived in my heart when I looked at you. a flower, any flower, wouldn't have been enough to capture an ounce of the whirlwind that lived within me at the sight of your eyes. I wanted to plant gardens of flowers in your heart.

You'd have known it was spring by the enchanting look of never-ending carpets of blue bells, the powerful fragrance of the hyacinth, the resilience of the puschkinia with its most extraordinary stripes and shades of blue, and the cheery trumpeted blooms of the golden daffodils. you'd have known it was summer when the petunias and the gaillardia would have fed on the warmth in your heart. the tickseed with its yellow and gold flowers would have bloomed again and again, until a chrysanthemum would pop up out of nowhere to announce it is fall. butterflies would have gathered around beds of purple and blue cartyopteris and you'd have known that no matter the season, there was always beauty living in your heart.

And all of a sudden, it would have been winter: you'd spot snowdrops here and there in the cold and lonely corners of your heart. in the places you never allowed me to enter, maybe out of self-preservation or maybe out of fear that I would not survive seeing what's inside. but, if the peonies are tough enough to survive the coldest of winters and then pop back up at the first sign of warmth, so would my heart.

I wanted to plant gardens of flowers in your heart, so it may bloom all year round and not just in the spring. so it may always remember me, even on the coldest of days, when most of the world is sound asleep, awaiting spring.

no amount of love
will ever be
enough
for the heart that is
not yet
ready to receive
all of which
you have to give.

I'm so tired
of constantly having to
water down my love for you
so you wouldn't feel like
you're drowning in it.
I am so tired
of

always being too much
and not enough
all at once.

sometimes,

love is

less about what we say,

and more about

what we choose to withhold.

silence,

does not reply;

although,

it is full of answers.

I am not a soldier, nor have I ever been to war. But I can recognize an ambush when I see one. And that's what I walked into that evening. It was the end of Spring and yet, it felt more like the middle of Summer. The tar on the roads was melting. I could smell the asphalt walking into the restaurant. Maybe I should have taken that as a sign that something cataclysmic was about to happen. But, I was so distracted by your eyes – mountain springs that I could see myself getting naked and swim in the whole night. Everything pulsed around you. You gave shape to a world I could never access in the company of another. We were having sushi for the thirtieth time that year. I didn't even know which one of us loved it more. I had borrowed so many of your mannerisms and I could recognize my own in you. A dinner after way too many lunches to keep track of; that was new. And while my cheeks should have bloomed flower displays looking at you, the tension in the restaurant was starting to steal the air from my lungs. Something was happening that I did not understand. Your gaze lowered and lowered. You were sitting so still…like a still-shot in time…and with the most heartbreaking look on your face you told me it was over. I'm sure that night, tectonic plates shifted somewhere in California. You were always an uncharted minefield, but that night, millions of broken pieces of my heart were left scattered in that restaurant. And as I left and looked up, like acid rain the sky fell on my skin. I died a hundred thousand deaths. I puddled an ocean as you were turning the corner and letting me flood all over. The horizon swallowed you whole, while I was still on my knees begging to know why.

While I was outside, it felt as though I was thrown in a locked prison cell with walls crumbling down and the room shrinking until I couldn't breathe anymore.

some days,
grief, wraps around
my shoulders
like a silky shawl,
on a breezy summer night.

the thought
of you
makes poetry
out of everything
my fingers touch.

for the lonely iris
the caterpillar breaks off a leg
as a keepsake.

you are the butterfly
and I,
the dreaming field of flowers
waiting
to be adorned
by your wings.

blanket of darkness –
the stars make longing
grow stronger.

my hope,
travels to you every night
it crosses bridges,
climbs mountains,
swims in oceans,
freezes through cold winds,
and braves the dry heat of the desert

only to fall trap
to a few abandoned leaves
by your front door
announcing proudly
that you haven't been at home
in days.

-no wonder every morning
she comes back exhausted

you've been a hope.
you've been a dream.
now, a memory…
and always,

too hard to remember,
yet, absolutely impossible to forget.

I don't know
what's harder to swallow,
your words or your tears,
once you realize there is
nothing left to do,
but move on.

she jumped off
the cliff of despair
not knowing
where she'll land,
but hoping she'd
grow wings
on the way
down.

you wear it well,
the necklace of silent wounds
you'd like me to take
for pearls.
but, *I see you.*
every day,
your inner light gets dimmer and dimmer.
I see specks where just yesterday,
the sun was blinding me
with the strength of his shine.
you're starving your soul
by giving it all
to those who not only choose to forget
what you've done for them,
but also minimize, dismiss
and even make you feel guilty
for not having given them more.
today,
give all this light
you've been spreading in foreign hearts
a home, in your own soul.
(you deserve it)

fresh rain
falls onto my skin –
it's Spring again.

I wake up with what it feels like the entire world being at war and churning inside of me. I go in the bathroom to cry on the cold tiles like I've done it a million times in the past to bring this intensity that's burning my lungs down to something more bearable again. But I forget this time I have children and suffering of this kind is not for the faint of heart to watch. After all these years, you'd think I knew better, but I don't. I still don't know how not to throw myself into the garbage every time a maybe rolls off your tongue. I still don't know how to believe I deserve more than a one day.

I deserve today. Right now. I deserve commitment and certainty.

But when you look at me like that,
I forget I deserve anything at all.
All I know is that you are back
and no matter how hard I try,
I cannot say no.

a woman in love,
will not leave until,
she has exhausted
every resource
available to her heart
in making you see
what you mean to her.

women,
are fighters,
until there is nothing left
to fight for anymore.

don't walk out
of
your own heart
in order to make room
for
someone else.

we've been here before
and from time to time
we return.
I've lost count of how many times
I've found my worth
only to lose it
in a split second
because of a look
or a smile from you.
and all of a sudden,

I find myself back on my knees
begging for scraps of your love
when just mere seconds ago
I was fully aware of the feast I deserve.

if I knew then
what I know now,
I wouldn't change a thing.
you and all this pain
were here to teach me
more about myself,
than happiness ever could.
all these lessons lived and learned,
have polished me
into the woman I have become.

and that is a gift
nothing and no one
can ever take away from me.

tonight,
open the windows of your soul
wide
and let all your deepest fears and doubts
fly out and get carried away
by the wind's strong breeze.
let them find their demise,
away from the purity of your soul.
they don't belong to you
and you,
never belonged to them.
get ready to respond
to your heart's calling
truthfully, courageously,
and without flinching.
get ready to witness your life
unfold into something
spectacular.

tonight,
give yourself permission
not only to exist,
but to start living
as only you know how.

I might not always
be able to be the sun,
but I promise,

I'm always worth the storm.

don't be hard
to get.

be hard
to earn.

A sense of internal peace and harmony does not come through the elimination of daily life-stressors and chaos; but rather, though the realization that we are made of such undeniable resiliency, that no matter what life throws at us and no matter how many times we fall apart,

we will always have the strength
not only to endure, but also to overcome
whatever comes our way.

I ran into you by accident
you – a curse,
maybe a lesson
I was meant to learn.
and yet,
I was the one who chose to stick around.
I choose this pain every day
and no matter how many times
I try to make you take the blame for it all,
deep down I know
there were red flags
that I chose to ignore.

who in their right mind
likes tiny yellow apricots
instead of juicy summer peaches
after all?

it is a terrifying thing
to watch love
walk in your direction
when you believe
you are not ready
to receive it.

in the same manner,

it is quite terrifying
watching love
walk away from you
when you are not yet ready
to let go.

I don't want to feel like a check mark on your to-do list. I don't want to feel like a chore. I don't want you to think the world will end if we don't touch base. I don't want to be the cause of your stress. I want to be what relieves you from it. What gives you life. What waters the things inside of you that have been long-forgotten...the vitamin ... the nutrient your body and mind are missing and cannot create on their own. I don't want to be or feel like a second choice, or an option, when I deserve to be the first...the one and only...I don't ever want to bring you more darkness, when there is so much light I can carry your way. I don't want you to set reminders or make notes of things I like...I need...I want you to stop thinking and start feeling...Everything I need is already in your heart. And it knows when and what to do and say...if only you'd let it...If for once you wouldn't hide behind piles and piles of excuses, reasons why things cannot be. No one wants to be another bullet point you need to get to at some point during your day. We all want to feel special. Acknowledged. Thought of. Not necessarily in the most profound of ways...But just because ... We all want to know we pop up in someone's mind throughout the day. Not because we were written down somewhere, but because we are so important... so valuable to that person... that their mind organically navigated towards us...And when things lose their fluidity... when it is getting hard to feel things organically...Maybe then...it is time for a break...for your sake...for my sake...for everyone's sake...Silence redirects us... Silence takes us back to ourselves...Silence teaches us what is important and reminds us of what gives our lives meaning and purpose.

Silence is needed when talking does more harm than good.
Nobody wants to be a checkmark in someone's planner at the end
of the day...
We all want to be thought of
...just because...

you are
so, so far away…
yet never far enough
to stop haunting
and tormenting me.

one of the bravest things
I had to do
was to allow myself

to be alone
with all these memories
I have of you.

I still don't know
who you are,
but I don't think it really matters
in the end,
for when we are together,
I know exactly who I am

-the best version of me I can be

some days
you're a razor
to my veins
others,
you're teaching me
about restraint.

I'm not your summer house;
nor am I,
your winter, fall or spring.
I am not a house at all.

(there is nothing temporary
about this heart of mine).

I am not a guesthouse.
I am a home.

like coming back home
after a long and strenuous trip
through an unforgiving jungle,

that's how it feels like
every time I am back into your arms.

your name,

sits too low on my tongue.

and nothing

that comes out of this mouth

is as exquisite as the stories

my skin would recount,

if it were allowed

to speak.

your first love is
unforgettable

until,

the love of your life
walks in

and makes it
forgettable.

Reminder:

it is always where
we feel most alive,
where we will find
our happiness.

on those days
you feel
particularly numb,
pull the sun closer
to your lips;
inhale its energy
and let it warm
your insides
with its heat.

the problem with arms

is

they get tired.

and they let go of the things,

the people they hold.

that's why

you should aim

to be held by hearts,

not arms.

for it is far harder,

to convince a heart

to let go of
what she loves.

lust,
used to
make me feel
so full.
now,
all it does is
leave me
empty.

some people,
are better left
in your memories.
your heart,
wouldn't be able to take
another round of
what they have
to offer.

We wait for things to get better. For life to get easier. Relationships to be less complicated. We wait for Mondays to get a start on things and wait for Sundays to have breakfast in bed. We wait for "next time" to say I love you and wait for tomorrow to be happy.

We wait, until we run out of time.
Don't wait.
Enjoy today for what it is and
put no expectations on tomorrow, for it might never come.
And if it does come,
allow it to surprise you!

your only responsibility is
remaining true to your own heart.

even if that means,
you'll have to inconvenience
some people in the process.

wrap my heart
in soft petals of consistency.
let all your promises wilt like flowers
and clothe this love
in bold, decisive actions.
bathe me,
in endless admiration
and nourish my soul
with empathy and validation.

and I shall give you a love
like you've never seen before
never felt,
never knew existed.

yet,

always found yourself craving for,
long before either one of us
even knew what true love was.

in the chaos
of life,
you are
the oasis,
the stillness,

that brings me back
to myself.

he cuts me open
with his words
and makes me
bleed flowers

There is so much that we can do with the love in our hearts: we can fill others and make them feel worthy, loved, cared for. A human being who feels important, who feels that he/she matters will always believe in the light at the end of the tunnel. So before you tell yourself you have nothing to offer to the world, put your hand over your heart and believe that is the best gift you could bestow on another.

Make someone feel important today (even if they do not see it, acknowledge it or thank you for it...) and you might not just change another heart, another future, but the future of humanity.

from time to time,

she makes herself heard,

the voice of the woman I was

when my heart got caught somewhere

between sunset and sunrise,

at odds about what to do;

follow the burning,

the ache,

the wild

in her chest

or leave it behind.

with the fallen autumn leaves,

and the dried out bread crumbs

the birds have long forgotten about.

and it is then,

that love's hand reaches out for me,

begging me to stay

for just another round.

-it will be different this time

what I crave the most
are samples of you.
small doses of the nectar
on your skin, tasted
in the middle of the night
as you roll over
and reach your arm out
to check if I'm still there.

If you want to convince me
of the beauty in your heart,
show me that
you can forgive.

two things
always in
my heart:

you and
spring.

if only for a moment,
I could make the entire world
disappear.
so that for once,
I'd have you entirely to myself.
and I wouldn't feel as if
I had to compete
with anyone or anything,

not even
with the rain.

fill my longing
with rose buds
and make me bloom.

in the darkness
of my thoughts,
forgiveness
lifts
the veil of
my sorrows
and ever so gently
I break
into millions
of luminous stars.

nothing
wakes my soul
quite like
the warmth
of your smile.

one word from you,
and millions of butterflies
grow wings
inside my heart.

forever trapped
in the melody
of every word
we ever shared.

I made a wish today.
I wished for you
and that's no different
from any other day.

we might not be
holding each other
tonight
or any other night
for as long as we live,
but while there is breath
in our chests,

we are still standing
under the same sky
and the stars will forever be
the witnesses of our love.

hearts change
when
eyes meet.

she had been struggling to find answers to questions that hurt. time had proven to be a disappointment in helping her forgive. forget. move on. then one day, as she was sitting in class, beautifully unaware of what was about to transpire, as if waking up from a dream-like state, she stopped. she stopped listening to the lecture. stopped listening to the relentless inquiries of her heart. stopped paying attention to the torments of her mind. and for a second she sat in stillness. in peace. in solitude. and then, as if someone had finally handed her the right glasses through which she could notice the world again, she slowly tilted her head, looked up and saw him. he had been there, right in front of her for months, and yet her unanswered questions about a past that had no place in her present or her future had been eclipsing her view. and as she glanced into those beautiful brown eyes, she knew. she knew *she was now free of the shackles of the past and ready to love again.* a gentle sigh escaped her lips as she quietly felt her worries melting away into the warmth of a new beginning now shining in his eyes.

and when I saw him
looking back at me
as if
he had been searching
for me
for whole lifetimes,
I knew
my waiting
hadn't been in vain.

there is
a tenderness
in him
that he refuses
to acknowledge,
but it was it
that made me
fall in love
with him.

I look at him
and I don't know
of reason.
all I see are
fairytale in his eyes
and wild on his lips.
and then,
all I want is
to press myself
into his skin
so hard...
that
it melts like butter
and lets me,

all the way
in.

he changed
my world
with
his smile.

I believe in
a dash,
a semicolon,
continuity.
I believe in
love,
not stopping,
fighting for what matters.

I believe in us.

love is more than a feeling. love is a decision.

you can't just stop by when it is convenient and call that love. true love stays; it stays through the inconvenient. when sadness hits, when the rain starts pouring down on you, threatening to bury you alive in waves of water and hail, true love does not become intimidated by the roughness of weather.

true love picks you up in its arms and shows you that you
are not alone in your struggles; it shows you that you are
important and that you matter. true love does not turn its back
on you when things get tough; it reaches for you in the dark
and pulls you towards the light.
true love stays, no matter the season.

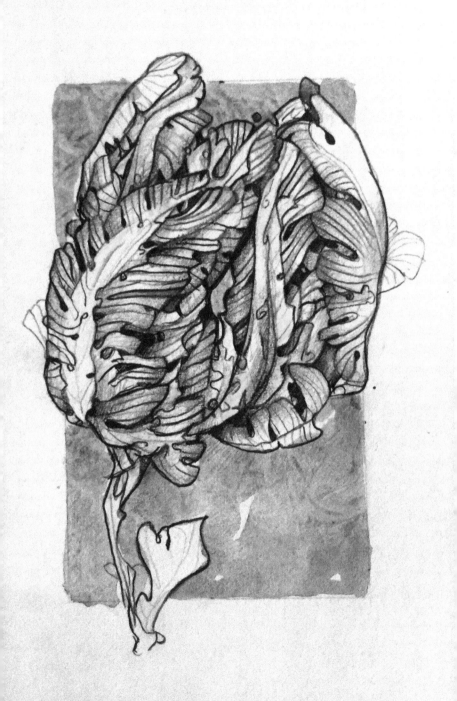

Most people wouldn't describe the best kiss of their lives having happened in an empty parking lot, after having sushi at noon. Most people would need a picturesque scene. They'd have you follow the crease in the hills with your gaze, hike to sights were you can pull the sky closer to your mouth and there…underneath a sky full of stars, lay you down next to a creek of quietude and murmur sweet words of love into your ears, before daring to brush your cheeks with their lips and then getting a taste of you. But we were not most people. We never needed perfect conditions to create the perfect atmosphere to be together. We spoke without words and when we were together we lived in our own snow globe. That afternoon, we looked at each other too long to be just friends. Sparks flew, and even the day was blushing at the sight of our love unfolding. I laid my head on your chest as if trying to memorize the rhythm of your heart. In many ways, I could feel this was not how it was always going to be. I tried to savor the moment for I knew it was going to depart soon.

You left that day with your heart full. I gave you an oasis,
yet you took it as a flood.

my love for you
is as pure and fresh
as the taste of
mountain water
in the middle of spring

my heart is a garden
of thoughts and feelings
turned into roses
and they all
smell like you

missing you –
a patch of sunlight
caresses my soul

morning wind,
sad cherry blossoms
breathe rain

waves of memories,
come into the cove of my mind
one at a time.

every night,
I cross an ocean of stars
to feel you
in my dreams.

I wish
I could cradle your face
into the palms of my hands,
and make you look straight into my eyes,
while I infuse,
every single fiber of your being
with the certainty that you are,
have been
and always will be

the one I hope to share
each and every one of my tomorrows with.

I long to be known by you.

Not in the way you used to know me. Not in the way I used to be when I thought that you'd only want me if I acted a certain way, if I said certain things or wore certain clothes. I long to be known by you the way that I am today. Right now. I have come a long way from who I used to be and have yet to climb mountains and walk through uncomfortable straights to get myself to where I know I want to arrive. But right now, this version of me is a testament of all that I have accomplished and all that I have in me to become. I long for you to know of my struggles, but also my resilience. I have been looked at for far too long as pieces, parts, fragments, droplets, moments. I am a whole. I am a Universe all on my own that you have yet to discover and explore. And I am telling you now that I am willing to allow you on board. I'm tempted to tell you of everything we could accomplish together, but I am resistant. I hold back. And this time, not because I don't think I am right or because I think I'm not enough, but because I know I am too much and I fear sometimes that going forward, I will always be too much of a woman for a man who doesn't know the importance of self-awareness. For a man who doesn't value empowering his partner by showing appreciation when it is due and by acknowledging his mistakes when it is appropriate. The things we could accomplish. The places we could reach...I could venture in their direction all on my own, but it feels like I should be looking back just one last time. And maybe this time, you will grab a hold of my hand...and maybe this time, you will not be afraid to hold on. And in turn, maybe this time, there will be a future for us, after all.

I long for you to know me the way that I am right now so you may see that future in my eyes every morning you wake up with a doubt peeking from under your pillow or a fear sneaking up from in-between the bedsheets.
I long for you to know that no matter the hardship or challenge, I will never let you go!

and the truth is,
ever since I've met you
I've spent more time
imagining
the life I'd have with you
than living
the life that I come home to.

I don't know how
to look at you
and act as if you're not
everything I wish for
in this life,

and the next
and the next...

It's Spring again…I'm 92…By now…

I have forgotten: my name, your name, the name of our children. And yet. The walk we took around Lake Vasona that Spring…When you nestled your hand in mine…and you rested your head on my shoulder…That memory is untouched…

I'm still walking with you around the lake…
and you're still holding my hand…and resting your head on
my shoulder… And it's Spring […]

Parting Words

My Dear Reader

Breathe in sunshine
Breathe out clouds
Breathe in hope
Breathe out doubts
Breathe in strength
Breathe out weakness
Breathe in beauty
Breathe out hate

May love, grace and gentleness
find their way into your heart, mind and life.
May you learn to appreciate the journey
and the struggles as much as the destination.
May you acquire patience and believe in
the immense power of the breath.

A world of endless possibilities is at
our fingertips while we are still breathing; it is all a
matter of time for them to make their way to us.

Acknowledgments

Although it is my name that appears on the cover of this book, the actual writing that has gone into making it a reality has been a collaborative process that has involved my family, friends, and even my co-workers. It truly takes a village to make a book come to life and I would like to acknowledge everyone's tremendous contribution.

It is difficult to define and quantify everyone's support, but I will try to do my best.

First and foremost, this book would not be here without you, my readers. please know that without your constant love, kindness and support, I might have stopped at book one. Thank you for believing in me and for investing your hard-earned money into making my dreams of writing a reality. I will never, no matter how hard I try, be able to express the gratitude living in my chest whenever I think of your kindness (but, if I were to try, I would encourage you to visualize a purring cat on a window sill in the middle of winter – looking out at all the snow and thanking the Universe she is inside, enjoying the warmth and safety of her home). Thank you for offering my words a welcoming home and for keeping your trust in me! With all this support, comes the tremendous responsibility to always remain true to my craft and write with an open and an honest heart about what moves me. Keep on reaching out! I will never tire of hearing from you! Never!

Secondly, thank you to everyone who listened to me and my endless rants about the difficult process of writing this book: Iulia Poenaru, Dana Coman, Marni Dieanu, Gloria Truong, Irina Constantinescu, Lisa Whalen, Deb Fujiwara, Katy Scott and everyone else who read my lines and responded to me every time I sent them new work or illustrations that were just starting to take form. I am eternally grateful for you! A huge thank you to my co-workers who have been incredibly supportive of my writing and buying my first book, following my journey on Instagram and sharing with me how my words made them feel. I would like to especially thank Sana, Peter, Kim and Joyce here. You continuously inspired me to keep working hard and not give up on my dream of writing.

Thank you to the amazing staff at the Starbucks shop that has started it all...and a special thank you to Rachelle and Ramina!!! Your coffee kept my mind awake and your words kept my heart warm...This coffee shop provided me with the music I needed to get inspired and stay inspired. Much Love to you!

A special thank you to Alina Roman for the beautiful photograph she took for the back cover of the book and also for her friendship along the years. Your support has been invaluable to me!

Beatriz Mutelet has done it again; she has created the most amazing illustrations both for the cover of the book and the interior...I am constantly amazed at her talent and professionalism...Words will never, ever...be enough to express my appreciation for her craft!

Thank you, Mitch Green for yet another job well done with the design of this book! I am already looking forward to us working on the next one!

I am forever indebted to the wonderful Molly Hillery who wrote the foreword to this book and who has been a constant supporter of my work since Day 1. Molly, you are a gem and a true angelic presence in my life. Thank you for your undying love and support! I am incredibly grateful for you!

My heartfelt thanks to Alfa for taking the time to write such an exquisite review of Unforgettable. Thank you for your time and friendship. I am honored to have you as a friend and so very thankful to have connected with you in this crazy world of social media!

My immense gratitude and appreciation to the wonderful Dawn Lanuza for her review of Unforgettable. I am still in disbelief sometimes that you took time out of your busy life to read this piece of my heart.

To Lynn Truong – Thank you for your wonderful support on my writing journey. I am so appreciative you took the time to read my words and share your feedback with me. Your encouragement means a lot to me.

To A – May we meet again some day…in another life…when we are both ready…

Last, but definitely not least, thanks to my family and especially to my patient husband without whom this book would not have been possible! I could not have made it this far without your undying support and am grateful for you and your love!

If I have forgotten someone along the way, you have my apologies…I promise to give you a warm hug when I see you!

I love you all so much and am very thankful for your support…

UNFORGETTABLE

About the Author

Madalina is a writer, mother, wife, and an aspiring psychologist. Madalina has always been a lover of books, words and creative expression. Originally from Romania, Madalina has published extensively in Romanian, but her bestselling book, Words Unspoken was her very first publication in English.

Madalina is currently working as an associate therapist in Northern California. She has recently graduated with a Master degree in Counseling Psychology and is preparing to apply to Doctoral Programs; she especially enjoys working with patients who have experienced grief and loss in their lives.

When she is not writing or doing therapy, Madalina enjoys spending time in nature with her family, planning vacations to new places she would like to explore, cuddling her cats or reading Cummings. Her favorite writing topics are love, heartbreak, grief, healing, self-compassion, self-acceptance and self-care.

At the moment, Madalina is working on another collection of poetry.

You can find Madalina on
Instagram: www.instagram.com/madalinacoman
Facebook: www.facebook.com/madalina.poetry
Twitter: www.twitter.com/mada_c

ALSO BY MADALINA COMAN

WORDS UNSPOKEN

CPSIA information can be obtained
at www.ICGtesting.com
Printed in the USA
BVHW011948270620
582324BV00009B/22